Nerve Energy
and
Psychic Phenomena

*

Essay

*

Traumear

*

Nerve energy, more commonly known as nervous energy, resulting from initially unavoidable resistance to our elemental environment, is to draw our attention to the wonder of world-experience. If we fail to deal productively or even creatively with that resistance, we are confronted, in ourselves, by psychic phenomena which in turn, unless countenanced, turn into psychosomatic, psychomental and psychophysical states – which in turn, unless dealt with – confront us as phobias, allergies and addictions. It is shown, experimentally, how all these apparently negative and even bad 'problems' essentially draw our attention to the possible removal of underlying blockages to human-natural growth.

*

Nerve Energy and Psychic Phenomena

How important is rest! If we cannot get what we sometimes call 'our rest' we 'feel out of sorts' or 'can't settle'. Rest is always good and never to be confused with self-indulgence on one side or peace on the other. When something 'disturbs our rest' we become angry and resentful. A restless spirit is upon us when the performance of some task attracts us. Then we might feel inclined to identify it as 'raw energy', which fuels creativity. We 'come to rest' in the evening or after our task is completed, when energy is invested or spent. Those who have died are said to 'rest in peace'. At least that seems to be our wish for them when we chisel RIP on their tombstones. Primitive man most everywhere was probably wary of the dead interfering with his calculations and plans, so he pleaded with them and bribed them to stay quiet and not get restless, like the natives.

Creative human beings, not at all dead, perhaps even live, welcome raw energy and they have learned how to cope with it. The creative spirit flares up in them like a blaze and it would not occur to them to quench that spirit in favour of 'a quiet life'. Neither would it occur to them to consider that this creative fire disturbs their rest. They are liable to feel perfectly restful while they deal with the raw energy welling up within themselves and looking to be embodied. The behave in such a way that due to this energy and on account of their creative will and skill a work comes to fruition. Such a work then is no less without than within themselves, so that while outwardly they build something that testifies to life, to truthful, beautiful and plentiful life, inwardly they construct a constitutional soul and all that pertains to it.

*

A psychic phenomenon we will be discussing at length in this essay is mimicry. Even in so-called nature, or 'the natural world', we come across much that is not as it seems, most ob-

1

viously perhaps among insects. The morphology of mimicry makes for an exciting and fascinating study. Though there are borderline cases, we rarely confuse animals with plants. What is especially important for our study is that we do not confuse human beings with animals. Human beings are spiritual entities, with souls, while animals are 'like' them and therefore not spiritual but – well, in short, animal. We humans sometimes like to pretend we have animal instincts and we like to think of 'primitive man', prior to the blessing of civilization, as largely ruled and driven by them and that is indeed a successful way of building our ego. But egos shun souls and the energies they feed on are not endless of supply but they become scarce and run out. In order for an ego to replenish its energy it must trespass, which is no good news for the trespassee. Shortage and surfeit of energy is an egotistic problem; the characteristic problem of the human being, by comparison, is the ego itself. No spiritual entity can abide self-centred entities; spirit is ever flowing from one to a few, to several or to many.

*

The trouble with nervous energy is that it comes and goes for no reason we can rely on. We should not be relying on nervous energy, that goes without saying, but we do it all the same, frequently in ignorance. It feels so nice to be 'energized', especially after we have been 'not really very well' for a time. So we build our hopes up. Then the rug is pulled out from under our feet. It was a threadbare rug but we didn't care. We imagined it was better than nothing. Certainly at the time it felt better than nothing. Now we feel cheated.

What is all that about? Is some part of us being held back so that another part can go ahead unhindered? Is nervous energy a kind of sop, to keep us quiet, or to make us look elsewhere for a time?

Certainly it looks as if our nerves alone were being stimulated; from within, of course. What we suppose we would prefer is that we ourselves were stimulated, not just our nerves. We would like the stimulation to be harmonious, regular and predictable, so that we can work and live. Instead we are fobbed off with 'something like'.

It would seem safe to say, at this early stage of inquiry that nervous energy is a deficiency, or at least a sign of a deficiency. We do think of energy in general as that which makes things move. We are in favour of motion and we deplore stagnation. Motion, flow, currency and circulation, these are desirable. Stagnation is unhealthy. Morbidity, torpor, lethargy and laziness – these are to be avoided. So more energy is considered to be good but when a child climbs the walls we are opt to say: "He has too much energy". Well-meaning parents want to tire their children out so that they can get them off to bed in good time. Then, of course, there is the 'energy crisis', macrocosmic, when coal, oil or whatever just makes the wheels turn and the rooms warm, runs out. Wood, coal and oil are 'sources of energy'. We burn them up.

This alerts us to the connection between energy and fire. The energy that is outside of us is spoken of as 'being harnessed'. By comparison, when energy flares up inside us we get jumpy, we look to 'let it out' on someone or something. Activities on the basis of inside energy has no other use than to tire us out. In other words it's useless and a waste.

How does energy get inside us in the first place? It's like an infection. Like a fever, which burns. We might like to get rid of it and even better, to avoid it in the first place. It's a sure fire in-dication, this inside energy, that there is an 'inside' to us, which was probably there before that useless energy moved in. I say 'probably' because I am feeling my way forward, into new terri-tory. It starts with an 'inside', with inside territory, then comes inside energy, useless or mere energy and then we get tiredness, wear and tear, torpidity.

3

So where 'insideness' comes into being, useless activity and business, and then wear and tear, are the consequence.

What is 'insideness'? Let's be totally abstract for a moment and compare 'insideness' to 'wihinness'. The former implies one of two aspects, or sides. You cannot be inside and outside at the same time. The difference is material. We can make that difference. We can turn a coin this way or that way. As for us, when something goes on inside us – rather than within us, say – it goes on in our material self. It either goes on there or we make it go on there. We can even decide to make things go on inside us. That is more than torpor then; it is turpitude. It is shameful and base. When 'insideness' happens to us, that is bad but we can take the responsibility for it as soon as we wish. When we actually decide to have this 'insideness', that is worse than bad. It is evil. We cannot take the responsibility for it because we don't have the required awareness. We have to be 'punished'. This 'punishment' is a good thing, because it alerts us to the evil we do, which implies 'isideness', which in turn allows us then to take responsibility for it.

While 'insideness' implies one of two aspects, in other words inside rather than outside, 'withinness', by comparison, means something quite different. Inside is separate from outside. You cannot look at both sides of the coin at the same time. Within me, however, is not at all separate from what is without me. Strictly speaking therefore 'withinness' is not even possible as an abstraction, because whatever goes on within me and what I do within me does not exclude the outward realm, which is world. Experience and action within remains open to what lies without, which is world.

The development of an inward realm is of crucial importance. Here we can decide to love, to hate, to care for etc. whatever we sense or opine at that moment. What we achieve in this inward realm, always open to world, overrides and surpasses whatever comes from inside or outside. However, unless we do in fact operate within this realm, it disintegrates so that we end up with 'insideness' or 'outsideness'. It would hardly make sense to say that we must sustain and manage this realm within, because while we do good, which is what this inward realm is for, it remains, and when we stop doing good we risk an 'isnideness' developing.

You might well ask – and I ask it so that you don't: Why bother with these special representations in the first place? Why not just say that when we stop doing good we start to go bad? My answer is: What we imagine, we have at our fingertips. Those who are locked up inside themselves or else astray in the outside world are without doubt undergoing a punishment, which is to say that their one-sidedness is being drawn to their attention. I use the word punishment here in the only way that it should be used, which is correction by others or by circumstances so that one becomes capable or responsibility for oneself. When we resent or reject this correction we are being vengeful. When the Lord says: Vengeance is mine, he is asking us kindly to mind our own business, which is the acceptance of punishment, gracefully if possible.

We like to imagine spatially, so why not make use of that facility as we approach the truth? It helps me to explain myself and I hope it helps you to understand.

Often, perhaps usually nowadays, what is called, or thought of and feared, as punishment is really revenge. People 'want to get their own back'. It's difficult to imagine what we really get back. If someone steals my car and then the police manages to get it back to me, I am getting my own back alright. But if someone slaps my face and I slap him back, how is that getting my own back? This is almost an interesting question. If slapping someone's face is a pleasure, very well then, since you had that pleasure it's only fair that I should have it too. It's the way poorly brought up children might argue about who has the most sweets. But surely harming someone is not a pleasure. Mind

5

you, if I am presently being punished, which is commonly to an extent a painful situation to be in, and a burden, then I might decide to offload some of that burden onto someone else or on my surroundings. For a moment I reject my punishment and feel sweet relief. It's the relief that comes with returning to my blind error and to my evil condition, prior to punishment. If I had my wits about me I would realize that revenge may well be sweet but that this is an evil sweetness, the sweetness of decay. When we suppose that justice is not done until the one who hurt us is at least proportionately hurt back, we are certainly locked into a very outmoded notion of justice. Justice is in fact not 'done' until the one who had hurt or harmed me wishes he had not done so and tells me that. If, instead of forgiving him then, I still want him hurt or harmed back, I do exactly what he did in the first place. And we certainly cannot force anyone to wish he had done good rather than evil.[1]

*

The previous thought: 'Those who are locked inside themselves or else astray in the outside world are without doubt undergoing a punishment' needs further explication. Being locked inside oneself is in fact a punishment. Gong to jail for stealing a sheep is the analogue for it. The 'penitentiary', or jail, should afford a thief opportunity for repentance. This is the analogue of the reality. After all the poor man might not have stolen the sheep at all, so that he has no misdeed to regret. Nonetheless he still spends time in what is called the penitentiary.

Turning to the reality of being 'locked up inside oneself' again, we can understand that this too is an 'intelligent punishment' for something, namely for not behaving in the way that is becoming for a human being, which is doing good. Stop doing

---

[1] It's difficult to imagine what sort of a rabble a law-giver would have to come up against to have to stoop to the likes of 'an eye for an eye, a tooth for a tooth'.

good and you end up 'inside yourself'. It's a gradual process, of course. The thief too usually gets away with swiping a few odds and ends, with embezzling a few millions, say, before being apprehended. He gets time to think it over, conscientiously. So in reality too. We might not be doing as much good as we could if we applied ourselves to full capacity, but this does not mean that we right away slide back into a complete state of 'inside' captivity, from which we have to be liberated by external agencies.

Nonetheless it is quite true, and it does make sense after all, that an inverse proportionality operates here. However we are at a given moment, this can be compared, theoretically of course, to how we would be if we were at that same moment doing good to our full potential. We can completely put the power we have – and power is always ability to do good – to work. We can do good work to full capacity. No one else can, of course, tell us what that full capacity is, but we ourselves can know it. Then, to the degree that we do not work to full capacity, we are 'inside' ourselves. We might also be 'outside' ourselves, and we will look at that in a moment. Right now I would like to concentrate on what it means to 'be inside oneself' and I want to compare this state to how we are when we are working well and to our full potential – and our potential should always increase, by the way, right up to the moment when we depart to return. (Leave that to one side for the moment as a mystery, this departure to return.)

Instead of saying 'do good' we could also say 'be human'. To be human is to do good and to do good is to be human. We can do more or less good, so we can also be more or less human. (We cannot be good or do human. This has to be thought over very carefully.)

Nothing could be more important at this stage than to realize that no one has the ability or insight to say how much good someone else should be able to do. This is entirely something for the individual person to decide for him- or herself. Not only can I

7

not decide, or know, how much good you should be able to do at the moment but I cannot even know whether or not you are doing good. But that is terrible, you will say. For years I have chided others for being bad to me. I have criticized my acquaintances, praised my friends, lamed my enemies. Are you telling me that was all blind flying in the clouds?

Afraid so. You were judging so that you wouldn't be judged and not judging rightly. You were praising your friends so that they would praise you and you were accusing your enemies so that they wouldn't accuse you. Don't get me wrong, so was I, of course. As a matter of fact I am really talking to my self here.

Being human and doing good is everyone's own business – what a liberating thought that is! Can you not feel your wings sprouting? No one can truthfully say to someone: a. That he is not being human, not doing good, or b. that he is not being as human or doing as much good as he might. If he says it anyway, and means it, he is transgressing. He is not only not doing good but he is being bad. Should we tell him so? Of course not, because we have no idea who that person is. What matters is that he means it and how can we tell what anyone means? Only you know what you mean and I know what I mean.

*

Being locked inside ourselves we worry about our health, for example. I cannot work because I'm sick. Wrong. I am sick because I'm not working. Ah, but it's a very specific kind of work that is meant here. Certainly not meaningless activity. Or what about the difference between hard work and working well? In the present context we can see that hard work will help to release us from our trap inside ourselves and working well will keep us released. It can be quite discouraging if we try to continue to work well if for one unfortunate reason or another we have got caught up inside ourselves, health-wise for example. When we work well we simply translate good spirit into testimony. True substance pours out of us like the proverbial river; at least that would be one way of putting it. By comparison now, if we work hard we are applying ourselves to some obstruction. Our spirit has come up against an unwillingness in ourselves and is asking us please to remove it. Inward effort is required. Not inside effort, such as concentrating on a pain or a pleasure – or the resistance of a pain or the prolongation of a pleasure – but inward effort, which does not exclude outward awareness. This hard work is called hard because we steel ourselves against something which continually or repeatedly seems to be trying to draw our attention to inside considerations, to a preoccupation with our self, our ego, our selfish motives and predilections. We harden ourselves against these. There are bound to be upsurges and abatements of this voice which for all intents and purposes says: Me! Me! Me! So we have to be on our guard and be willing to work hard until a natural transition allows us to work well, again or for the first time.

We have arrived at a position now in our proceedings where we should be able to define our topic. Nervous energy and psychic phenomena were mentioned. The psychosomatic phenomena we just at the moment described. They are what draws our attention to our self, ostensibly to prevent us from escaping from inside entrapment by working hard.

However lets not make a modern devil out of something for which we ourselves are responsible. These psychic phenomena do not 'have it in for us'. The best way forward is always when we recognize them for what they are and then we work hard to remove ourselves from their clutches.

What should we concentrate on, in order to work hard? It's all very well to tell someone to work hard when by that he understands nothing else except repetitive, gruelling labour. Hard work is not mindless work. No force is involved. This is especially important, that no force be involved. The phenomena at the mercy of which we seem to be are in themselves forceful after all and by being forceful ourselves we would only be playing into their hands. So what do we concentrate on, when we work hard?

Our brain. Brain activity is what counts. Have we another word for brain activity? Cerebration? That would do. How do we cerebrate? How is that different from straightforward thinking?

The inner eye comes into its own here; that with which we practice insight. It is an organ in its own right. It has to be developed and then maintained, through use, like all our organs. Not our mind but our spirit is active. Even those who are poor in spirit have what it takes to develop this organ. Especially those who are poor in spirit, because they are less likely to be sidetracked. Only once this organ is developed can we really distinguish psychic phenomena. It comes into being counter-actively to those phenomena. Which is not to say that this happens accidentally. It is we ourselves, discountenanced by those phenomena, who spiritually pit ourselves against them, again not by meeting force with force but by countering force with good spirit.

The name we give to the force which these psychic phenomena 'mimic' is nervous energy. We can certainly identify this energy when it wells up in us, either lethargically or enthusiastically. More fittingly it would be called nerve energy and that is what we will call it from now on.

When first we develop this organ of cerebration, specifically of spiritual insight, which we called the inner eye, that is 'hard' work. What has to be withstood and counteracted is something that is facile and volatile. We needn't kid ourselves, it's not a task we can accomplish without discipline and dedication. Mind you, we do have a spur, because the alternative is illness for which there is no medication and sickness for which there is no real relief. All 'addictions' and allergies are of this nature and their motive force is mimicry. There are allergies and addictions of the body and of the mind. The more attention we pay to them and the more time we spend deciding what we are addicted and allergic to, the less time do we have for counter-action them insightfully.

We have a choice when it comes to cerebration. In addiction to the inner eye, as the organ of insight, which is one species of cerebration, we also have the inner voice, as the organ of speech.

A lot of what I come up with here is not entirely new but I have never seen it presented in this particular shape and form. It has been known for centuries, perhaps millennia, that much of what we call illness and sickness, mental or physical, cannot be explained in terms of some material surfeit or scarcity. Whether any sickness or illness at all can be explained this way once we divest ourselves of materialist and spiritualist convictions and beliefs we leave to one side for the moment. The alternative to a belief in miracles is a tragedy of the modern spirit; when we say that something is miraculous we mean that it cannot be accounted for by the laws of nature and that may be correct as far as it goes. However let us not confuse the nature of the scientist and of those who 'believe in science' with human nature, which is spiritual reality in person and beyond laws. This human nature, from the point of view of the scientist's nature and its mechanisms, forces and laws, is miraculous throughout. So the simple fact, the simply horrible fact, is that those whose believing stops with materialist nature will have nothing to do with human nature, neither within nor without. When they say human nature – and of course anyone can say anything – they mean a few predictable popular customs and habits, whereupon it becomes increasingly difficult, as some superstitions dwindle and others take their place, to differentiate in any meaningful and persuasive way between so-called human beings and – well – animals, for a start.

It is therefore seriously incumbent upon those who know human nature in truth and understand it in reality to work hard and well to present their knowledge and understanding in as many ways as possible so that human nature and those in the possession of it will not be entirely discountenanced.

11

Why do those who have it in them to question their existence do so time and again, as if it were not enough for them that time, space and causality regulate the world? They always become such gadflies and then of course social man turns them into scapegoats

This need no longer be so. A language exists nowadays which simply cannot be grasped by people, however they are not provoked by it. Human beings meanwhile know it as their meat and drink. It is the language of true speech and it forms itself on our lips. Its principle characteristic is the quality of understanding. We must know when we speak it that no one will associate what they know with what we say. At the source of this language is the human brain and from there it draws into communication all the parts of our constitution, namely flesh, spirit, soul, body and mind. It would never do to limit its effectiveness to some particular end we have in mind. In other words it would not help us win an argument or entertain an audience. The truthful expression of it is that of prophesy and for that reason we may plainly call it prophesy – as long as we keep in mind – and perhaps remind ourselves now and again – that it tells us nothing about the future. In fact it tells us nothing about past, present or future. Its work relationship is the realm of the eternal.

What we called the inner organ of speech, or voice, comparable to the inner eye, produces this language, so we do well not only to keep our eye clear but also our voice sound. This can be done in a variety of ways. The way that probably gives the best results is writing. When we write from this inner organ of speech we automatically dispense with all psychic phenomena, and nerve energy can make no inroads. It may however build up in part of our constitution upon which we do not touch, so our aim will surely be, little by little, to touch on all parts of our constitution. What we need therefore is unlimited access to who we are.

This access is not readily available. It is one thing to know that I am. This is extremely worthwhile knowing because the god who is good and merciful dwells in my being. Knowing that I am means knowing that merciful good spirit dwells in me. It is quite possible, and even likely, that those who question their existence are taking the first step towards that knowledge and that merciful good spirit has in fact begun to approach them so as eventually to dwell in them.

Only then, when this spirit begins to dwell in us, can we also begin to know who we are, since personhood begets personhood. Merciful good spirit within us defines our personality. Prior to that we may suppose we know who we are but in fact we define ourselves, and we do so in terms of internal or external phenomena, which we mistake for reality.

*

When we speak of phenomena we mean whatever appears to us in whatever which way. The world of phenomena is therefore no world at all because there is neither plan nor order but it is like a collection of stones from the beach, some like this, some like that and others quite different again but all of them with rounded contours where they have been rubbed against one another, some perhaps for a million years or more but all interesting in a way, as if each, in spite of being so much like all the others, nevertheless had its own story to tell and were eager to tell it.

Psychic phenomena then are pebbles which we classify because we suppose we can see they have something in common which is less evident in the others. Let us say they are all not of an even colour, slate grey or pink marble, but completely speckled. Once we have come to a decision about this characteristic we can sort these phenomena out from the rest. No, not from the rest, not at all, and this is so important that we should never tire of repeating it on occasions when we suppose there might be an ear to take it in. Not from the rest then but – from the innumerable, uncountable many. And let us use the word uncountable in the strictest sense, not in the sense that there are so many of these phenomena that we would surely tire before we had them all counted, which is, after all, the case with pebbles on the shore, because at any given moment there are a definite number of them – on the earth, shall we say, for that is our limit.

No such limit exists for phenomena. All we can say is that now we shall occupy ourselves for a time with phenomena which share this characteristic of being psychic, some very much so, others to a lesser extent. Even some of our pebbles are less speckled than others, though all are speckled.

What, then, is the telling characteristic of the psychic phenomenon? It is this, that we know it as part of ourselves when it fact it is not. So although knowledge is involved, it is not reliable knowledge. We cannot say that this is so and there is an end to it.

At the same time it would be quite wrong to call these phenomena false. They occur to us for a definite and legitimate purpose. If they did not, then a closer look would identify them as false.

When we do take a closer look, what we come up with is self-knowledge. Self-knowledge is not knowledge of myself, of me as the person I am and as merciful good spirit defines me but of my self, as I am not but seem to be.

I can get quite involved with this self-knowledge and then I can be said to be selfish to that degree and extent. I am not selfish because I think about me and not about others but because I believe these psychic phenomena, which come upon me unasked and leave unpredictably. Why they do so is less important than that they do so and how we can cope with them unselfishly.

*

Our first contact with these phenomena is such that we mistake them for being real. As we try to behave accordingly however we find ourselves in a situation where certainty is impossible. Even if we do feel certain, then, if this feeling is a psychic phenomenon, as soon as we try to build on this certainty, it turns out to be the exact opposite, namely uncertainty. We feel warm and as soon as we relax we feel cold. We suppose we have mastered something and no sooner are we gratified than what we imagined we had mastered falls to pieces.

These phenomena do not reveal themselves for what they are until it is too late to ignore. Time and again we are tricked into credibility and just as often we draw mistaken conclusions. It wears us out, this incessant back and forth, between puppy love and ferocity, between reliance on our self and reliance on someone else, between pain and exuberance.

The idea is that our brain as such should begin to function. We are presupposing here, and quite correctly, that some kind of life can go on in a brainless sort of fashion. I have referred to the 'brain as such' advisedly. We all know by now that the frontal lobe does one thing while the cortex is responsible for another and the medulla whatever helps us to focus on colour and to identify the opposite sex. That is fine and dandy as far as it goes but when we add up all these parts we do not come up with the whole but only with a hole, a black sort of hole, which is then projected out into the universe and weighed down with the responsibility for explaining this and that.

We are besieged and bedevilled by psychic phenomena so that we will learn to use our brain as such. It would not be a bad thing if we simply began by wanting to do so. In addition to this we might know who we are because this knowledge draws on whole brain activity. The thought: 'I am someone' combines readily with the wish to use our whole brain, as an organ in its entirety.

So it seems we have to choose a moment when we are not just affected by nerve energy in order to consider that we are someone, while we wish to use our brain, i.e. to cerebrate. We

15

can wish to use the muscles of our arms and legs and we can want to use our eyes, so why should it be so difficult to wish to use our brain – except because we have so rarely if ever done it?

*

Nerve energy on its own is identifiable. Stimulants set it in motion. Then we feel excitable or dull, one or the other, depending on the state of our constitution at the time. Conventional nerve energy is not associated with dullness; we think of a 'nervy' individual as of someone jumpy and on edge. However that just means that the energy is on the outside, where we can all see the consequences. When this energy occurs on the inside, our senses, instead of being agitated, are suppressed, and this we experience as lethargy.

In both cases we are being affected against our will or in the absence of our will. If we think of our will as spiritual appetite or as our spirit in action, then any affection contrary to or in the absence of our will is bound to have a very one-sided effect on us. What is undermined by it right away is human natural affection because it depends on our entire constitution, including this rather central element, our will, being moved.

Stimulation is a crucial factor in all this. We are stimulated entirely or in part. We are stimulated from without or from within, form outside of inside, internally or externally. Human-natural affection is inward stimulation of our entire constitution. When I am stimulated human-naturally I am totally involved, not just some part of me. Nerve energy is partial stimulation. Our nerves are telling us that we are not being whole. They cannot tell us what part of aspect of us is being stressed or neglected but only that we should be pulling ourselves together. "Pull yourself together!" we say when someone is being affected by nerve energy. The nerves pick it up when we disintegrate. How utterly confusing this can be to someone else! Nerve energy changes our very personality, so that someone will say about us: "He was quite changed," or "He was beside himself." "I am not myself," I will say. "I am all in the air," or "I cannot come to terms with myself. This torpor is killing me. I don't know what makes me feel so heavy. I shall look for a diversion, entertainment of some sort."

*

Psychic phenomena are never what we expect them to be. This makes it almost impossible for us to isolate what we mean by them. Certainly illusion is involved. They appear to be like something we know or have known. That is the element of mimicry. The question is, will we be taken in by it? On the other hand, can we afford to ignore them? Should we perhaps learn how to mimic back?

What we commonly call art, is that not a kind of mimicry? Is art not the successful way of dealing with these phenomena, especially once they have begun to get on our nerves? Imagine creating figures, faces, landscapes and what not for no other reason than to make sense of the irritating back and forth of our tortured nerves!

If art transforms, then it changes psychic into realistic phenomena. Realistic in this case means reminiscent of reality. And reality is singular. Every leaf on a tree, every hair on your head, is singular. Every leaf on every tree, every hair on your head "is counted".

That which is psychic is nothing like that. Psyche is not our soul. It is the complaint, the grief, the agon of your soul when our soul is influenced beyond its present capacity by the spirit of merciful love.

*

Psychic phenomena are simple enough because they show up as negative feelings, emotions and passions. It is our mind that registers what is going on and so we cannot see as clearly, feel as deeply, sympathize as readily. Body is being negated because mind is preoccupied with psychic energy. What might

17

just as readily, or, to be honest, under other circumstances, have occurred to us as an increase of experienced human-natural affection is instead sidelined in the sense that our mind is agitated, stimulated of affected pure and simple, at the expense of our body. You might say that more goes on and we are less able to see what it is. Impossible to say which comes first.

We can deal with psychic phenomena by practicing a craft. We build something, make something with our hands, hopefully something beautiful and useful. Our body comes into its own again. Power increases beyond our previous power.

It is a one-sided, a lop-sided, affection which we call *psychic* phenomena. It is after all not only the mind at the expense of the body that is affected. It may also be the body at the expense of the mind. Then our mental faculties diminish. Sight, feelings, passions – i.e. visions – are so much more vivid and intense while thought decreases.

The mind wanders while the body undergoes a paralysis or the body loses its bearing while the mind is handicapped. These are all called psychic phenomena. Love, in terms of consideration or compassion, is the remedy in all senses. Easier said than done. These psychic states are infectious.

*

It should perhaps be emphasized that we can spot psychic phenomena only in ourselves, not in anyone else. This is because a degree of judgment is involved and we cannot in truth judge anyone else.

On the other hand, this is the first thing we tend to do, when nerve energy arises in us, that we judge someone. The spirit of criticism, comes into being. We are then of course responsible for harbouring that spirit. It works like this: First we ourselves are judged, from within, in terms of nerve energy. We don't like that at all and we want to get ahead of it and to prevent it, so we let it out in the open and judge others. We judge so that we will not be judged. This is a useless exercise of course. It

18

only makes matters worse. The benefit which was our due, due to being judged, is lost by us because of stubbornness, rebelliousness, presumptuousness, arrogance and the like. When we judge so as not to be judged, when we criticize, when we invite the spirit of criticism into our midst simply by making room for it because we do not behave mercifully, then judgment, which was intended for us as a boon, turns into punishment, which is also intended as a boon, as a benefit or something that is intentionally good for us. The only realistic difference between judgment and punishment, as it arrives on our doorstep from within, is a degree of pain.

I fully realize that this equation of judgment with nerve energy is a new development in this essay and it deserves to be taken seriously. The ethical dimension of our human constitution is all-inclusive and certainly the most interesting.

The fact that from time to time we are judged from within may not be an altogether familiar one, especially not to those for whom the various elements of our constitution are wholly material. What does judgment mean, after all? Does it not mean a restitution of balance: a reestablishment of equality where equality is life-furthering? So why should we flee from judgment?

Well, of course we don't. what we flee from, understandably, is the pain involved. If we always knew that this certain kind of soul-pain were a consequence of being judged and that judgment is beneficial, sure wouldn't we have much more of a courageous go at suffering this pain rather than reacting to it and fleeing from it?

So it all depends on what we have learned and what we have learned to practice.

Most important, I suppose, would be the recognition of *soul-pain*, as such. Then we require as much as possible of self-knowledge, by which I mean knowing how readily we are willing to offload this pain onto the person next to us or onto some aspect of world. Then we need to know about mercy, because

19

mercy alone, practiced by us in this case, will aid and abet the judgment that is so painfully upon us, thereby precluding the pain which we have begun to suffer instead of demonstrating our aversion to it.

Remember that our search here is still limited to psychic phenomena, as caused by nerve energy, and that we have not yet turned to psychosomatic phenomena. Which raises the question hypothetically: Should we not also expect psycho-mental phenomena? We may come back to that.

*

Soul-pain at its very beginning is a mood. When we are *in a mood* we have the first indication that an increase of merciful good spirit is upon us, or, mythically speaking, that god has moved closer to us. It may be a 'good mood' or a 'bad mood', that makes no difference so far as our reflective understanding is concerned. We know from plentiful experience that pleasure is not necessarily a sign of something good happening to us.

So a mood is the beginning of judgment and our recognition of moods, timely if at all possible, aids and abets the judgment or process of repair that is upon us. When god approaches us, when good spirit influences us, it frightens us, momentarily at least. We jump. We are shocked. We react. We behave in an unpredictable and irrational fashion. Our basis for existing as we have existed until now is called into question. It cannot be otherwise. We can fool ourselves by supposing that a good mood is a sign that god loves us whereas a bad mood is a sign that he does not, but that is nonsense. Both good moods and bad moods are signs that god loves us, sure enough, but primarily, or let us day: more immediately, they are signs of our rebuttal of that love – and of god's available mercy, of which we may avail ourselves by *suffering* these moods, good or bad. God, in other words, on such occasions, not only loves us more, practi-cally speaking, but at the same time holds out to us the means of coping with that additional good spirit (which we experience temporarily as a good or a bad mood).

If we do not confront these moods, patiently and with understanding of course – or we might say: lovingly – then we get involved in something that is more complicated and more painful, but the elements of judgment and punishment, of rebellion and mercy still are part of the equation. Certainly it is in our interest, however, to deal intelligently with moods as they come along. Elsewhere I have referred to religion as the science of moods, where science is knowledge for the sake of understanding. Religion in that sense always involves judgment and mercy, while it is by no means the prolongation of a good or even a bad mood. The suggestions that such a prolongation has often been called, and is still nowadays called, religion is not far-fetched. It could perhaps be called modern religion inasmuch as it testifies to a lack of thoroughgoing ethicality.

*

What complicates moods for the untutored mind is what complicates all psychic phenomena, namely that they are both and at once signs of our rebuttal of good spirit and merciful opportunities for repair, specifically for religion. The two prongs of the tongs with which we handle them must consequently be repentance and mercy. Inwardly we may repent of our aversion while outwardly we show mercy. By showing mercy we make room in ourselves for mercy to operate. By repenting we prevent any further involvement in denial or betrayal of merciful good spirit. True religion is fundamentally always both repentant and merciful, while those who preach rebellion and self-righteousness only aggravate the problem.

*

I am in a good mood and everything is going swimmingly. How do I know I am at risk? In other words, once I know how dangerous a good mood is, how can I identify that I am in one?

21

Am I not most likely to feel thankful that I may be 'happy' for a short time and make the best of it?

But that precisely is the question – how to make the best of it; which is not to try to prolong it. Noticing it is of course important from the start. And I suppose what we may notice in a straightforward fashion is the carelessness of our being and behaviour. Sometimes we even 'couldn't care less'. It's a telltale sign. However we do miss it. We have been known to miss it. So we go on for a while in our selfish happiness careless of others too, not just of ourselves. We are especially careless of those in our own home. Why? Because familiarity breeds contempt. Also these people owe it to us to be kind and friendly and not to tell us the truth, to expose us to the truth unnecessarily.

Then the punishment comes, which is merciful good spirit's way of alerting us to the danger we are in and offering us a way out. Should that feel pleasant right away? How can it? It is bound to be painful – but only to the extent that we are committed to our good mood. Only to that extent does the person, the individual, who becomes a tool of this punishment become our enemy. Of course he is our enemy, since he (or she) disturbs our self-satisfied mood. Our worst enemies are in our household – but only to the degree that we have become a social unit, contractually obliged to support one another in happiness and therefore to guard one another against the truth. If we think of the truth as a harmony of the spheres, then our mood should tell us – is to let us know – that we have fallen out of that harmony and that the 'Erynnies' are upon us to bring us back in. Will we resist them?

It would be the height of foolishness. Yet we do it. I do it. Sometimes it seems to me that I am particularly slow on the uptake and I don't know why that should be. Is it work-related?

It's amusing, but actually sad, to see how some who have repeatedly fallen out of their personal harmony and into a good mood and then experienced the dire consequences – how they work themselves up artificially into a bad mood, to avoid the consequences. When we do that we are liars, of course and happily good spirit is not fooled. We mimic the bad mood, meanwhile continuing to be careless inside. We pull a long face on every cheerful occasion. We call that playing it safe.

And what about the other side of the coin? We pretend to be happy whatever mood we are in. That particular lie is more prevalent in societies where being happy is more popular. Being happy, or above all appearing happy, is the obligation placed upon the member of that society to guarantee his membership. If he feels down in the mouth, there is social pressure on him to hide this behind the mask of a happy face and demeanour. Meanwhile the cancer of that bad mood eats away at him.

And there we have our first indication of how the *psychosomatic state* develops from out of a psychic condition. We also have an indication now of how there must also be something that should be called a *psycho-mental state*. That had not occurred to me until just very recently.

When we insist on persevering with our previous being and behaviour once we he have been painfully alerted to the fact that this being and behaviour is psychic – that is when the psychosomatic state (or the psychomental state) sets in. In other words, we do not heed the merciful punishment but instead we resent it, (or ignore it). Body (or mind) is abused in the service of subterfuge. With our senses we repress (with our thinking we justify) the wrongness of our being and doing and as a consequence it turns bad. The step from wrong to bad is both crucial and deplorable. I mean deplorable in the strictest sense. Our psychic conditions we can deal with within ourselves. Our psychosomatic states have to be worked out outwardly. Bad being and behaviour, due to our wickedness in other words, calls for *confession in the community*. This present essay, for example, is just such a confession.

*

23

Love of the truth is never a waste of time. We can do it both inwardly and outwardly. That's what's so nice about the truth, that nowadays we are able to love it both within and without ourselves. I only mention that because those who cling to modern times will passionately disagree with me. It's true nonetheless, that we no longer have to hate, anyone or anything, in order to love the truth.

So why is that so good for our soul, and consequently for the rest of our constitution? First of all it has to do with how and where love originates within us, namely in me or in you. Not in our constitution, therefore, or in some part of it. It originates in me or in you, in him or in her. Have you ever tried to say that in another way? I have. I got nowhere. The witch-doctors always come up with the ego, the self, the I, as something you can shake a stick at, but it isn't I or you, him or her (he or she). It is merely the agent of survival. If I let it, my ego will place survival at the top of my agenda. I don't want it there. Life belongs there. So sometimes I have a bit of a struggle on my hands. My ego knows nothing of life. Life is the forbidden fruit on the tree for it and it prides itself on being ever so law-abiding. It will kill to abide by that law. It would kill me if I let it. Those who commit suicide, even they are killed by their ego.

It cannot bear the truth, my ego. Neither can yours, by the way. It will argue and justify its selfish law until it's blue in the face if only the truth can be made to appear not to exist. That is all it asks. Love of the truth is anathema to it. It goes so far in its struggle against the appearance of the truth that it mistakes it for accuracy – on purpose. This is hard to believe. It seems unfair but there is absolutely no need to believe accuracy. It can be measured. Comparison can be made. Limits can be drawn in the sand.

So now that we know where love of the truth comes from, we have to ask: What is it? Can it be described in some way, for the elucidation of those who need two or three versions of a

24

thing, clinically distinct each from each, before they venture forth to shake it by he hand and risk smiling at it?

I don't say love is one thing and truth is another and then the two can be brought together by us. To say that would be a travesty of the truth. Rather, love of the truth is what I do when I am entirely who I am and I don't care who knows it. Of course I have to know that that is what I do. It's a gentle stirring of the heart an the head while I am who I am. I cannot lie, in that situation. If I wanted to lie I would have to become someone else. I would have to side with my ego to a degree. I would have to let my ego come into being to a degree. I would have to believe that there is such a thing as my ego. No longer being who I am, my heart and head would no longer be entirely my own but to a degree they would belong to my ego, which is nothing more or less than an accidental imitation of myself.

A gentle stirring of the head and the heart while I know who I am and what I do – will that do as a description?

Love of the truth – how can a psychic state develop in its proximity? How can nerve energy even arise? And when it does, how can it possibly last? And if it did last, would we not at last put a stop to it?

*

Love of truth – or love of *the* truth – is there any difference? One myth after the other falls by the wayside as we make our way into mature human being. Truth is a word and words change as they leave our mouths. We don't ever need to wonder what we meant when we 'speak truth', as the captain of a ship on the way to the island of Dia off Crete repeatedly put it. "I speak truth," he said. "The water is clean. I drink it." He meant salt sea water and I believed him. I have to watch myself now, else I will disappear into a dream. The hot scent of oregano on the rocky hillside – the sun overhead, not burning except if you ignored or resisted it – the horizon like my wife's eyes, always half and half but not always noticeably so.

25

What are we talking about? Ah yes, nerve energy and psychosomatic phenomena. We had just decided there must also be psychomental phenomena. Let's recapitulate. If we don't take our punishment, mercifully dealt as always, then this might be described as: We don't see sense and we don't take thought. We do neither. In order to deal with our psychic phenomena, within ourselves, we have to 'see sense' or 'take thought'. Either will do. Either body or mind. A physical response is out of the question, since this is all going on and being done within ourselves. So we will exercise either a "gentle stirring of the heart" of a gentle stirring of the head, whichever seems to suit at the moment. We are being judged, and to the degree that we have stepped out of line we are being notified and helped out, both. Nobody can step out of line if he's dead. Everyone does who is the least bit alive and desires to live and to have life. Before any of this can apply we must assume the venture and the quest. We must assume human nature and the desire to grow, to mature, to bear fruit. We are not concerned with those who want to exist for the sake of existing, who want to survive for the sake of survival, to propagate and proliferate for no other reason. If there is no ethical will, no will to do good, to serve other human beings, then all this we say must seem like empty talk.

Our main concern and interest in this essay is, however, not psychic but psychosomatic and psychomental phenomena. They come into being when we do not exercise that gentle stirring of the heart but instead we harden our hearts and refuse the just punishment and the mercy that motivates it, so that our body gets involved with our psyche. They come into being when we do not exercise that gentle stirring of the head and instead we become headstrong, so that our mind gets involved with our psyche. Because we did not see off or think away those psychic phenomena which occurred inside ourselves, internally, we find ourselves now in a disadvantageous external situation, where others and world are involved. On that account I would add a third dilemma to 'hard hearted' and 'headstrong', namely 'stiff-necked'.

*

Psychosomatic phenomena arise due to the fact that we resist psychic phenomena with our bodily faculties. If we resist them with our mental faculties we end up with psychomental phenomena.

Nothing could be simpler, but where does it get us? Stop resisting in that case, you say, and these phenomena will all disappear. Suddenly we realize it's not so simple after all. On one hand this habit of resistance may be deeply ingrained in us, so that literally we resist without knowing. If we do not know it, how can we stop? Evidently we must get into the habit of doing something that overrules those 'bad' habits. We might as well take it for granted that we are beset by those bad habits of resisting psychic phenomena. If we were not, then a stroll through a crowd or a conversation with someone, or even an afternoon spent in pleasant contemplation of sky, earth and universe will end in such an accumulation of resistance that we will wonder what we did to bring on subsequent misery and malaise.

So looking for where we resist and then stopping it is not the answer. Much better to ask: What are our body and mind really for? What are he operations of our soul, as they manifest in terms of body or mind, which aid and abet our human being and how can we cooperate with these? For our soul is a human soul, forever active on our behalf, just as an animal's soul and a plant's soul are active on their behalf, and if the argument about souls should suddenly rear its hoary head, then yes, animals and plants etc. have souls, but they are animal souls and plant souls, whereas we have human souls. We can confidently let animals and plants etc. continue to be responsible for their particular souls, as long as we are responsible for ours.

Don't forget that all this knowledge will come in ever so handy when the modern craze for a manmade world will have run its course. Then there will be ample time to reflect on who we are and why we are around. Meanwhile it seems like a good idea to prepare for the shock – so that it will be less shocking. We do in fact have what it takes for a smooth transition.

*

We have identified three types of nerve energy. In addition to psychosomatic phenomena we have discovered those that are psychomental, when we resist psychic phenomena with our mind. We described these further as being hard-hearted and headstrong. To these I added the predicament of being stiff-necked.

Now when we are stiff-necked, this is the most unfortunate of those three conditions, because our resistance of nerve energy is not bodily or mental but both; in other words, physical.

We have discussed in detail elsewhere how our soul seeks to manifest itself so that we might cooperate with it. Initially we have no notion of how to do this, so that body and mind must become independently distinct for us. Only then can we begin to see and think intentionally rather than being at the mercy of a welter of opinions and sensations. Then, once our mind and our body have become distinctly familiar to us, as the two sides, or hands, of or soul, we can begin to behave and act physically bringing mind and body together in unison. At such a time we are also liable to resist psychic phenomena physically, with vision and conception in unison, and that is called being stiff-necked. A stiff-necked person is capable of perception, by which I mean that he or she has what it takes to be physical, which is to say mental and bodily in unison, but refuses an increase of perception and reacts with antipathy to good spirit on those physical terms.

As we indicated to an extent earlier, while psychic phenomena testify to internal resistance, because the merciful good spirit we resist approaches us from within, any resistance, in turn, of the psychic phenomena misleads us into the external realm, where we are, it is true, twice removed, in a way, from that inward merciful good spirit. Since love of truth originates within, any denial of that spirit ends in a domain of internality, or brings about such a domain, which mimics what should be the realm within. In the same way does any flight from this inward judgment produce a domain of externality, and of course it is twice as hard to find our way back to truth from that external domain, which mimics the realm without, or the outward realm. How terrible for us, if there were not available for us a help in that external domain to which we may address ourselves in our predicament. It occurs to us, or presents itself to us, as myth and as history; not as any old myth and history but as the personification of god and his entrance into the world. These two are assurances for us that we need not be permanently lost and continue to go astray in this external domain but that we may immediately open ourselves to this benign and saving influence.

The fact that merciful good spirit occurred historically in person and is available today mythically is the good news and the blessed reality without which we would not wish to be. Knowledge and experience of this history and myth transports us out of that external domain into that same outward realm in which we would have landed if we had not resisted psychic phenomena. Or lets put it this way: The outward realm, which includes the inward, is as readily obtainable from the external domain of psychosomatic, psychomental and psychophysical states as it is from the internal domain of psychic states. What counts, of course, is that we actually avail ourselves of this help whenever we need it.

*

The history of merciful good spirit in person is documented in a way that leaves much to the imagination, which gives it its

29

strength. The myth of that spirit is accessible to anyone who approaches that realm truthfully.

What we have to ask now is, how does anyone in a psycho-physical state come up with the wherewithal for learning true history and for appropriating real myth? Once I am lost out there, the outward realm is closed to me. It might as well not even exist, for all I know or all I can tell. I have built my world around those psychomental states and they are what I believe and what I believe in. Even if I said I believed in God and meant it, I would still be believing in a psychomental state.

Something from that outward realm would therefore have to leak into my psychophysical domain and it would have to draw attention to itself in a way that could not be explained on my psychophysical terms. It would have to be inexplicable to me and initially I would try to pretend nothing strange has happened. Eventually whether or not I managed to cope in some useful way would depend on my grasp of true history. I would then seek to match up my really mythic experience with my truly historic insight and 'make something out of it'.

However I am in the same predicament with respect to true history. How can I have 'a grasp of true history while I am stuck in a psychosomatic system? So even on that score I depend on something happening to me, something unforeseen and indescribable in relation to my attitude to the past and here too I am bound to behave, for a time, as if no such thing had happened. I say 'for a time', and no one can say for how long someone whose 'story' has been invaded by 'strange' facts or whose 'belief system' has been undermined by 'unusual' experiences will persist in denial.

On a strictly mechanistic level the outward realm (including the inward) composed of true history and real myth, and the internal and external domains (separate from each other) are mutually exclusive. While you exist in the latter (or insist on it) you cannot have any notion of the former and while you live in the former you certainly have a good idea of the latter and therefore will have none of it.

Human beings, however, are not machines. They are liable to mechanical behaviour and to mechanistic thought processes but their essential humanity, far from residing in these, abhors them.

What we have to look at therefore, as we hope to find an escape route for our 'totally inhibited and handicapped being' are the ethical determinants of psychosomatic, psychomental and psychophysical phenomena and states, which we have named and described as hard-hearted, head-strong and stiff-necked. They seem to sum up just about everything that can go wrong with us. No one is born like that but we are born with more or less inclination in that direction, so what we are really looking at here is the threefold domain of our wickedness. We define wickedness as our liability to be bad and therefore to do what is bad.

Does it really come down to that, then, that in order to set out on the path to life we have to consider our wickedness? We have to acknowledge that we are liable to become hard-hearted, head-strong and stiff-necked?

It looks like a valid point of view. It does not, however, sum up our human nature. It merely indicates a crucial and inarguable aspect of it. I am wicked, among other things. I am also noble. But nobility is the exact opposite of wickedness. It is the liability to do good and to be human. Wickedness, by comparison then, is the liability to be bad and do what is popular.

I know that 'liability', as I use it here, is a loaded word. Mankind has wrestled for millennia with some of the meanings it suggests, both traditionally and linguistically. How often is a perfectly legitimate and potentially fruitful problem not swept under the carpet ever so deftly by the use of a word full of meanings! On the other hand how often is a single word not responsible for dislodging a thought from a brain cell that had to all intents and purposes died many years ago, such as before the flood!

*

There is no doubt that any free human being is always at liberty to choose between wickedness and nobility, between popularity and humanity. He is liable to be the one as much as the other and as a consequence of urgent searching he will always be able to distinguish between the two. Any help we can give one another on that score should always be simple and straightforward. What would seem a little less obvious is how we set about helping someone who is caught up in psychosomatic states and for whom psychomental and psychophysical phenomena have taken on a reality of sorts. We know that for anyone who is trapped internally or lost externally, a call must come from within or from without, which is bound to cut across that individual's pattern of belief and experience and which cannot be denied or resisted for long – not because it must eventually win out and persuade him or her to truth and reality but because at that stage which we might call the third stage of good spiritual influence, that individual's very individuality is being judged and if he or she insists on being hard-hearted, headstrong of stiff-necked then that individual him- or herself is effaced, is finished and at an end.

The first resistance, practically unavoidable, leaves us with psychic phenomena. The second resistance condemns us to psychosomatic, psychomental and psychophysical phenomena and states. The final resistance leaves us with nothing, so that we have neither nature, nor personality, nor individuality. The third and final judgment wipes us out unless we know at least by now how to obey the command of love.

What we can do for others, then, at whatever stage they find themselves, is to love them unconditionally, not so that judgment and punishment will be removed but so that they will be effective as quickly as possible, since the reason for them in the first place is not to hurt and harm but to resurrect. And the resurrection of an human being is a glorious process indeed.

Something should be said about the resistance to which I keep referring. If we don't have some image of what it means to resist then we will be 'against it' even while we're doing it.

To understand the nerve energy that is generated as resistance we must have some notion of true rest – or of true peace and real rest. In comparison to such rest, then, the resistance which is nerve energy becomes conceivable.

So for example we perceive that we are not in the full possession of our faculties while we resist. That part which we do not 'own' does the resisting. It's a simple enough insight, which persuades us that the onus must be on owning as many of our faculties as possible, thus minimizing the occurrence of nerve energy. Also, whenever nerve energy occurs, we can take it for granted that more faculties are 'up for grabs'. Surely an increase of power is always attractive. Who would not wish to be able to do more good! As we must never tire of repeating, doing good is the maturing and fruit-bearing drive of each and every human being. The urgent search for more potential and greater capacity for ethical being, behaviour and action is surely what defines 'the human being', in comparison to any and all popular conceits.

What about the following approach: Before we can know and understand world-environment, we must have <u>mind-presence,</u> <u>body-consciousness</u> and <u>soul-awareness.</u> We must be inwardly more or less sound before we can become outwardly effective.

Imagine someone now who is fifty years old, say, and resides in a middling size town in Germany. He is married to his third wife, has 'fathered', loosely speaking seven children, was born in Nairobi, has dark skin, brown eyes, black hair, one metre eighty-one tall, brought up in a village by missionaries, etc. etc. Do we know him? Not at all. We know a little *about* him. We can only guess at what his attitude might be to music, to his wife, to white-skinned protestants, to his job, to nomads, to

33

German nationals, and so on, ad infinitum. All this has to do with world-environment, either directly or indirectly. If we wanted to get to know him, in person – and it must be in person if it is to be knowledge – we would have to talk to him, above all to listen to him, to his opinions, convictions and judgments, none of which would necessarily have anything to do with his world-environment. People live all their lives at the foot of a mountain and they have never really seen it. This may be either because they are clueless or because they have too much to see that is justifiably more important to them.

When we converse with our man a little we discover that he feels he eats too much. Now we begin to know him. We know both that he is able to feel and that he feels he eats too much. He may in fact eat too much, at mealtimes or between, say. There is such a thing as gluttony. However he may also be wrong about that. Who can say why or how it occurred to him that he eats too much. Enough said that when he sits down for a meal he right away fears there may not be enough for him and unless he eats as much and as rapidly as possible he will come short. Again, this might be so. In that case he is astute to think as he does. However, he informs us, food shortages, where he lives, are a thing of the past. There is always more than enough and yet he secretly fears there might not be. He sounds as if he might be open to some improving suggestion, so we tell him that whenever he sits down to a meal he should rest a moment and remind himself that there is more than enough food. This means that he has to deal with some nerve energy in himself. When he sees food, his appetite flares out of all proportion, even though previously he was not the least bit hungry. Available food means to him he must store up. This is like a short-circuit in the brain. A crisply fried chicken may make him feel grateful to a degree that such a thing exists, but to a greater degree he fears that there may not be enough or that someone may run off with it.

To a degree he <u>resists</u> the potentially nourishing presence of the crisply fried chicken. Why might he do that? What is the cause or reason for it? On the other hand, is it necessarily useful to know that, if he is to help himself or to be helped? Modern existence is morbidly overburdened with explanations of a sort that are ethically pointless. They lead to the knowledge that "puffeth up". We tell our man to go on a diet and behold, he puffeth up even more; after a while to be sure.

So when it comes to the crunch, what our man really and truly needs is not the force to resist that chicken even more than he already does, nor an explanation for why he sub-consciously resists it in the first place, but the ability to accept it wholeheartedly and to trust that it's there for him and for no one else. That increased trust will heal the rift for him between conscious and sub-conscious being. Increased confidence will allow him to be entirely grateful instead of greedily glad and fearful.

*

This resistance is initially accidental but it can be organized, and then it becomes problematic. What we do well to learn is that at first sight of it, of the nerve energy which eventually implicates various puzzling illnesses and diseases, we can understand what is going on and act accordingly. Our world-environment lets us know that something is amiss – not with it but with us. Someone has it in for us. We are not earning enough money. We have a persistent cough we would like such disturbances, or whatever cause them, to be removed. Only suddenly it occurs to us again that the fault lies with us – a fault in the sense of not rising to the cause of an inspiration that is potentially good and merciful.

*

The practice of mind-presence, body-consciousness and soul-awareness is crucial, of course, if we want to come to terms as quickly and intelligently as possible with psychic phenomena and states and with the nerve energy that inspires

35

them. Since we can never know ahead of time when good spirit will specifically address us, it would seem that 'readiness is all' here too. The resistance to good spirit, which we describe as nerve energy and which accumulates, unredressed, as psychosomatic, psychomental and psychophysical phenomena and states, is, after all, spirit too and we would not be smart to fudge that issue. Confronting spirit as though it were something else, such as matter for example, always leads to disaster. We remove symptoms and ignore causes. We kill the messenger and ignore the message. We throw the baby out with the bathwater. Our own human spirit is in fact truly our own only if and while we initiate ethical action and overcome hindrances to it. If we mistake spiritual hindrances for material hindrances, our spiritual initiative will not come into its own and we become spiritually deaf, lame and blind.

Mind-presence, body-consciousness and soul-awareness do not necessarily involve world-environment and there is no reason why they should while we are inwardly not yet quite sound. The inward harmony of our constitution is a priority. While we apply ourselves in the interest of this harmony, of its institution and restitution, we certainly deal with the general effect of world-environment on ourselves but it would not yet be wise to countenance the various and specific instances of world-environment themselves. If we did, we would run the risk of 'reading into things' what we can face only within ourselves and eventually of course there is always the risk of extinction when all of our internal concerns are projected into 'this' or 'that' world. Then we would be 'lost'.

*

Our initial response to world-environment is always and again wonder. Is it not wonderful that we can be out here in the light of day! Of course world-environment is in itself wonderful, I shall explain in a moment how I mean that. In the meanwhile we may be assured that every wonderful experience of world-environment comes up against an aversion of one sort of another in ourselves.

So we have world-environment which is wonderful in itself and we have wonderful experiences of world-environment – to which our mind, our body or our soul reacts unfavourably.

This is not we ourselves who react unfavourably to every wonderful experience of world-environment but our body, our mind and/or our soul. Matter resists the creator, that is unavoidable. Matter is in itself particles of resistance, which we have long known.

Why do we react unfavourably? Again, what would be the point of going into that? It would only satisfy our morbid modern leanings. Instead let's learn to recognize these reactions and to deal with them creatively.

First we do well to remind ourselves that we ourselves are not affected, but our mind, our body and/or our soul, in other words our constitution, is in revolt. I am not my mind, my body or my soul. I am who I am and that is my riches, my wealth. If something goes wrong there, I am responsible because I am in charge, for good or ill. So I don't get annoyed, I don't become frightened or resentful, please, because let's face it, my wealth is about to be increased and is that not cause for gladness? Therefore let me be exceedingly glad. This is like being glad in spite of feeling down-hearted. Because I am experienced and knowledgeable – because I have learned a few things – I can handle my affected or infected constitution creatively rather than being whelmed by it. Be moody as long as you like, I say initially, that won't make *me* moody. Then I do better than that. I quietly suffer that moodiness, in the knowledge that my constitution is strengthened thereby. Its aversion is transformed into acceptance.

That is how it goes if all goes well. If I ask for help I will get it. If I search for a solution I will find it. My ambition must not be to rid myself of the abhorrence or of the antagonism I feel

37

but to profit from that wonderful experience of world-environment. It may be a struggle. A worthwhile piece of work requires some effort. It may even be my lot and privilege to demonstrate this creative process for others, so that they might be encouraged to behave maturely and not immaturely. All it takes for them sometimes to escape from their 'selbst-verschuldete Unmündigkeit', as Immanuel Kant called it – from their immaturity for which they themselves are respon-sible – is to see that creativity actually works.

If instead we get involved in our reactive constitution we end up with phobias, addictions and allergies, and these can kill us.

*

World-environment in itself is wonderful, as we said earlier. Behold, it is so! Behold the cloudy sky, the material earth, the starry universe, it is all wonderful. It is available for us to be-hold when the inward harmony of our constitution is estab-lished. All our materialistic cause and effect reasoning, to-gether with its accumulation of forces and mechanisms, has fallen away and we stand safely exposed to the glory of the creator in his creation. We may have experienced this in art, which prepared us for the reality.

This is the environment in which we can do good without means-testing, if I may put it that way. Due to our soul-awareness we are able to process immediately the psychic be-ing of those in our vicinity. We do not even have to identify it, not to mention criticizing of judging it. In other words we are left free to love at our leisure.

Soul-awareness after all is not limited to an awareness of our own soul but the door to all souls is open to us. The essence of all beings is accessible to us to the degree that is appropriate to us at that moment in our working life. Not that our own soul is somehow mystically merged with all souls. Not that we stand in some magical proximity to all beings which allows us to control them for bad or good. Not that we have some mysterious hold on what 'makes things tick' which allows us to stand back from them with dispassionate contempt. No, what makes our position so enviable is that for once nothing inhibits the powerful unfolding of our spiritual growth within ethical parameters. It is enough for us to be, to do good and beyond that we can do all the good which present strength and circumstances allow

It should not be too difficult to understand that world-environment is wonderful and glorious in itself and that it does not stop being so once we stop perceiving it to be so. Paradoxically, it is not the beauty of the world but the power to perceive it that is 'in the eye of the beholder'. Of course we are not limited to an aesthetic perception here either.

Not until we have experienced the glory of world-environment in the flesh, however, can we properly appreciate what goes on when that glory is rejected by something within us, or when something within us gets in the way of what we might call the unavoidable but mistakable influx of world-environmental substance. If would, by the way, be absurd to suggest that no such substance exists. Again paradoxically, we might speak of the sacramental substance of the elements, as long as by sacramental we mean that which aids and abets our wholeness and perfection.

When the impediment is specifically psychic, and when it is psychophysical rather than psychosomatic or psychomental, what we have on our hands is a **phobia**. A phobia lets us know that in relation or reference to world-environment we are psychophysically compromised and that a greater power of doing good is available to us to the magnitude of that phobia. We know how personally crippling and socially embarrassing a phobia can be and no one in his or her right mind would not rather be without it. Think of this too as primarily a growth hindrance. It is a check on the communal unfolding of our natural resources and a stumbling block in the way of our pro-

39

gress towards mature personality. Calling a phobia an irrational fear is quite accurate as long as by rational we mean a description of how all beings as such relate.

*

The best way to tackle a phobia, once we have identified it, is to impress ourselves intensely and artificially with that fearful occurrence or state. Someone may have an irrational fear of appearing in public, perhaps of performing some skill in public. Even thinking about it makes him shudder. Let him then entertain a lively image of himself appearing in public, doing what he is afraid of doing there, and let him entertain that image with an intensity so strong that it becomes impossible for him to visualize it. The disabling character of a phobia is tackled in this way. Since the impediment is psycho-physical, the purging of it must be physical, so that body and mind, feeling and thought, are equally involved. He does this artificially, because the phobia prevents him from doing it in reality under those specific circumstances appearing in public, in front of an audience, say, or just plain facing a group of like-minded people, causes a separation of his body from his mind and prevents the two coming together physically, hence that jittery, uncontrolled feeling and that interrupted, unpredictable thinking. His body and mind are suddenly no longer truly his and as a consequence he is helpless.

The underlying phobic terror in this case is that of the human being faced by people. One could call this 'the' underlying phobia, on which all others feed. Humanity and popularity are, as we know, mutually exclusive. Human being is ethically centred in 'the other one', while popular being (actually a contradiction in terms)) is centred in the self. One self alone is only theoretically possible. In reality it takes several to lean on one another. People come in groups, in crowds and multitudes, whereas human beings are individually substantial in community.

People will always conspire to annihilate human beings and it is up to every individual human being to make this work for himself. "When they persecute you, be exceedingly glad," – that sort of thing.

So a phobia can be quite a crippling hindrance and the irrational fear of people is the most crippling one of all. A merely intellectual approach or a merely emotional appeal will not serve to deal with the problem. What is at stake, after all, is our physical wholeness, so that vision or conception alone remain powerless or even aggravate the situation.

We can learn to erect a kind of firewall, so that popular presuppositions can no longer harm us. However the damage that was done while we were young has to be undone. While most phobias come into our being while we are children, they may lie dormant until we come of age and try to think for ourselves. Then we come up against these inexplicable obstacles to our active behaviour.

For every phobia overcome, an experience of world environment is guaranteed. Gradually all our phobias are magnified for us, one after the other, so that we may exploit them. The elimination of the last one is usually a cause for celebration. Once people no longer make us nervous we can relax about that and much else falls into place. All the same when we realize how divided we are in ourselves, frequently, for no other reason than that our human endeavours interfere with our popular strivings, so that we cannot make up our minds whether we should 'love to hate' or 'love nonetheless', then it comes as no surprise when we discover how long it takes to remove such complexes as these phobias from our system.

The irrational fear of people is not the same, of course, as the irrational fear of other people, so we have to know where we stand. Is it conceivable that the popular contentiousness, for example, when the one who shoulders the other out of the limelight cannot wait for the same to be done to him, could be mistaken by him for something he would like to be rid of? Or is it possible for him to care for the wellbeing of the one who threatens his mode of survival? No, these are not phobias, for the simple reason that we must be rooted in rationality, as beings who would rather commune with other beings, if we are to fear irrationality, which is the concourse of things with things.

In retrospect then instead of thinking of phobias as irrational fears, we would do better to view them as instances of fear of irrationality. We can no longer afford to think of human beings as rational animals, nor of people as irrational human beings. Our study of phobias makes that clear. People will not let human beings live. The very nature of popular survival, which is popular nature, forbids the law of love which alone serves to prolong human existence. Love of enemy is essential if humanity is to thrive. Since people are the natural enemies of human beings, human beings must love them or else be forced into abeyance by them. And a grudging love will not do. In fact how human behave towards people can be a kind of test case for human love, since this love is not real until it makes possible for us an attitude towards people that is perfectly tolerant and generous on every instance and in every case. We cannot be polite but we must not be impolite. We cannot be kind but we must not be unkind.

So what we have learned is that a phobia is psychophysical hindrance to our human-natural progress in the face of – or in terms of – that world environment which is substantially wonderful and glorious experience. We have also learned that our fear of the irrational, i.e. of people and popularity, is the fundamental phobia from which all others spring. It would make more sense to call it not the fundamental, but the main phobia, because it is after all precisely the lack of foundation we fear. World environment is elemental and its unavoidable influx highlights or pinpoints those areas in ourselves where more foundation is needed – to support more life. Phobias, allergies

and addictions all testify to such a potential increase of fundamental strength. Then we experiment. We hold ourselves in
readiness. We cheerfully choose between paths without sign-
posts. And we overcome the various phobias that have taken
hold in ourselves during the intervening years.

*

An **allergy** is a psycho-mental blockage. It might be possible
here too to identify the main allergy from which all others stem.

If we have any competence of mind it is bound to reside in
our ability to think freely. In other words we can think without
apprehension of consequences and within limitations we have
imposed on ourselves rather than struggling with superstitions.
Sadly freedom of thought is not handed to us on a platter but
we have to gain and regain it. Neither is it the same as liberal
thought, which flaunts its lack of apprehension and admits of
no limitation, imposed by oneself or otherwise.

Any psychomental hindrance would therefore first of all get
in the way of free thought. Initially we might not even recognize that this is its purpose. It may start as an innocent enough
seeming pleasure, such as what we get from disporting ourselves liberally in the open air, of from skipping from one particular interest of fascination to another without bothering
about worth or value. We either avoid thought altogether or we
flirt with it and reject it. Thinking, however, is as important as
breathing. Also it can be done well or poorly. From rising in
the morning to bedtime in the evening we may be exposed to
such a welter of unfamiliar experiences that we simply cannot
rationally cope with them all. Some we reject outright, some
we store for closer attention another time if possible and still
others we may embrace with irrational vehemence. Superstitions and prejudices set in. These are only as serious as we allow them to become. They are more or less accidental. However they mount up. A particular experience rejected often
enough will turn into a hardened prejudice. This is no longer

43

just a hiccup in our smooth mental functioning. Other experiences, laid aside under the pressure of events and intended for scrutiny some other time, are forgotten about until such raw material accumulates and turns into an actual blockage in our subconscious being. That is how superstitions come into being. We tend to recognize them later rather than sooner. They become confirmed. The same goes for those experiences we embrace with rational vehemence. If this happens often enough it becomes a kind of trigger which forces or relaxes our thought. Once again we are at some appreciable disadvantage.

These hardened prejudices, confirmed superstitions and habitual prepossessions are disadvantages only in comparison to free thought. Meanwhile however our human-natural predisposition to mature free thinking continues to be effective, to act on our behalf, as it were, if we but knew. We are being urged to overcome those hardened prejudices, those confirmed superstitions, those abnormal prepossessions. As in the case of all beings, health always strives to assert itself and as soon as we work along with this human-natural striving in ourselves we attain to wellbeing. Health is a being's inborn state and unless we assume a certain dynamic in the direction of health where that state has been disturbed we cannot properly come to terms with the meaning of wellbeing. This is nothing new to those healers who understand beings as more than a set of lawful mechanisms. If we simply suppose that beings are healthy until they become ill and then, if possible, they must be brought back to health, we are rally not dealing with beings at all but with things, devoid of spiritual growth.

The main allergy, then, is the refusal, on our part, to espouse free thought after the event of prejudice, superstition or prepossessiveness. We are reluctant to think freely only to the extent that we would rather stick with that psycho-mentality. Just as the phobia is mercifully to save us from an eternal existence in the shadow of glorious world environment, so is the allergy to deliver us from fettered thought. Understanding is required. Not health but wellbeing must be the province of the healer. The attitude towards phobias, allergies and addictions is of course crucial. Make it cheerful rather than doom-laden. Without doubt the victim is to be pitied.

*

How can it matter that we are allergic to this rather than that? It does make sense, and we should expect it I suppose, that a falsehood should attach itself to something out there, in the hope of ascertaining credibility for itself. The same happens in the case of a phobia, that a fear attaches itself to something out there. When we come to discuss *addictions* we are bound to arrive at the same conclusion. Fears, falsehoods, evils all gravitate towards extinction and we must take care not to accompany them but to choose instead the here and now.

However we care less about how or why this extinct attachment takes place and more, much more, about how we might go ahead to choose the here and now instead. Of course we might be so absorbed in some addiction that the evil of it does not occur to us, especially if those around us are similarly addicted. The seeming righteousness of numbers misleads us.

Addiction as an evil not only presupposes the assent of our will or intellect, but our body is involved. We call it a psychosomatic aberration because vision, all the senses, feeling, emotion and passion are all at risk. A body of knowledge is our most precious possession and the source of our power. In the absence of such a body we cannot do good. Also it is the justification of such a body of resourceful knowledge that we do in fact do good.

So there again we satisfy a perfectly human natural instinct. The need to love brings our mind and our body into physical union so that we become personal spirits with a soul. Our desire to think would be satisfied so that our mind may indeed be ours and ripe for physical union. Our wish to do good, on the

45

basis of knowledge and wisdom, must therefore also be satisfied so that physical union and the blessedness of it may succeed in good time. These three human natural instincts will not be thwarted with impunity. The 'punishment' alerts us to where the shoe pinches, so that we may help those instincts flourish here and now.

An addiction, the way we use the word, is a psychosomatic hindrance to good behaviour and action. It is not, however, a hindrance to good intention. Hence the Tantalus torture experienced by the addict. He means and intends good but ends up having done evil. To help the addict we must take account of his good intention. Up to that point he is true to his instinctive nature.

*

Addiction – by which we mean evil addiction or addictions to evil – set in where space is left for them after an intention and before the execution of that intention.

Imagine you want to do good by caring for someone who is in trouble. Pity attracts you to that person. You have grown up in a culture where pity is lauded as a virtue and where a feeling of pity is readily mistaken for a helpful act. You will therefore try as well as you can to project that feeling of pity towards the one who needs help. You get quite good at it and eventually make a habit of mistaking projections of this feeling for doing good. Your human nature assents to that 'outlet'. Your human-natural need to do good, like all human-natural energy, will flow as best it can under the circumstances you make available for it. You do therefore experience some pleasurable satisfaction because you intend to do good. At the same time you are bound to experience a hateful dissatisfaction because you are not after all guiding that stream in the direction in which it is meant to flow.

The ethical urge, the need to do good, is born into us. Unless we admit that, we cannot satisfactorily explain why the pleasure we feel while we intend to do good is then accompanied by self-loathing if we do not after all carry our intention out. Of course opportunities will always exist en masse for duping ourselves. We might throw ourselves ever more energetically into this hypocritical, pitiful activity, hoping that by piling on the intentional pleasure we will drown out the self-doubt. That cannot work. But now we are in the grip of a fully fledged addiction. Our ethical intention was combined with force and now we are in the grip of that force. Any partial aspect of our body may be involved – or 'hooked'. Someone may have a vision of goodness and he settles down with it. He describes it, he adores it, he clings to it. For him that vision is his god. The fact that the vision is not made to culminate in action by him does not occur to him as detrimental. He may become a supremely unhappy artist or moralist or theologian because he experiences his human-natural dynamic of the ethos as perfectly genuine but what he does, his work, does not allow that ethos to unfold here and now in the light of day.

Similarly good sensations, or a sense of the good, is always praiseworthy. Often children are praised, both at home and at school, for being good children because one can tell they have this sense. Do we praise them for having two arms and two legs too? We are born with such predispositions. They are not achievements. We shudder to think how much evil is perpetrated when we praise 'good little boys' and 'beautiful little girls'. Why should a girl bother searching for that inner, ethical beauty for which she can be responsible, if she is made to feel that by being born beautiful she has arrived? Why should a boy bother about finding out how to do good if his parental adults lead him to suppose he can be good?

An addiction to good sensations makes us utterly intolerant and conceited. And of course we want to feel good. Good feelings are worth their weight in gold. More money, but then more money again, guarantees us good feelings – and always at the

47

end that feeling of emptiness. Good emotions, good passions – same thing. We can make them come about temporarily, even for one another, so that we seem to have a body. How hard we are willing to work to make seeming appear real, until it seems we can do no other. Then we are addicted and our body cannot come into its own. The intention is there; the execution, alas, is out of the question.

The sooner we face up to the disappointment at the end of the line, the better. Our human-natural ethos resides in it, negatively, of course. If we are addicted to feeling good, the good work is much more possible while we feel bad, not to put too fine a point on it. A period of dryness is unavoidable. However in its own good time the good work will bring its reward. Then we will be in no doubt as to the fulfilment of our human nature.

All the negative psychosomatic phenomena are ever so important because they contain the key to somatic success. These phenomena show us their negative side because we mistook them for realities and so that we might work out those realities. The nerve energy that comprises them is indeed difficult to countenance. However we have one who can ease us through those difficulties. His being is historic and mythic at once. He was and will be and therefore he is. Without him we can do nothing because our difficulties will always loom larger than our capacity. Those who know him know him and those who do not do not.

* * *

January 17, 2006